minimalist rooms

Laura O'Bryan

minimalist rooms

THE ART INSTITUTE OF CHARLOTTE
LIBRARY

An Imprint of HarperCollins*Publishers*

Author

Laura O'Bryan

Design and typesetting

Manel Peret Calderón

Texts

Eva Marín Quijada

Translation

Mark Holloway

Production

Juanjo Rodríguez Novel

Copyright © 2004 Atrium Group

First Published in the United States by: Harper Design International.

an imprint of HarperCollins Publishers

10 East 53rd Street

New York, NY 10033

Fax +1 212 207-7654

www.harpercollins.com

In Association with: Atrium Group de ediciones y publicaciones S.L.

Ganduxer, 112

08022 Barcelona

Tel. +34 932 540 099

Fax: +34 932 118 139

e-mail: atrium@atriumgroup.org

www.atriumbooks.com

ISBN: 0-06-059922-7

Library of Congress Control Number: 2003117142

HarperCollins books may be purchased for educational, business, or sales promotional use. For information, please write: Special Markets Department, HarperCollins Publishers Inc., 10 East 53rd Street, New York, NY 10022

First Printing, 2004

Printed in Spain

PHOTOGRAPHERS

Juan Rodríguez, Eduard Hueber, Ä. Lindman, Patrik Engquist, Jordi Miralles, Hans Werlemann, Tony Baggenstoss, Andreas Rubin, John Hall, Gregory Goode, Eugeni Pons, From Design Architecture, Paul Warchol, Koji Okamoto, Joan Mundó, Volker Sedieng, Tiggy Ruthven, Kisho Kurokawa Architect & Associates, Richard Davies, Hiroyuki Hirai, Henry Plummer, Yoshio Siratori, Pete Warren, Emilio Conti, Hervè Abbadie, Ricardo Labougle ■

ARCHITECTS

A-cero arquitectos | *Conceptual Spaces*

Aires Mateus & Associados | *Cubists Structures*

B&E Baumschlager-Eberle | *Adapting to the Surroundings*

Claesson Koivisto Rune | *Coexistence Between the Past and the Present, Rocks from the Desert*

Cho Slade Architecture | *Open Spaces and Intimacy*

Eckert Eckert Architekten ag | *A House on a Slope*

Francesc Rifé | *The Outside as an Extension of the Inside*

From Design Architecture | *Simplification of Space*

Gabellini Associates | *A Duplex Apartment with Views of Downtown*

GCA arquitectes associats | *The Fluidity of Space*

Hiroyuki Arima + Urban Fourth | *Volumetric Geometry, A Gallery Viewpoint*

Joan Llongueras, Jaume Alba, Jordi Mercé | *A Workshop Made into a Home*

Johnson Chou Design | *Classical Purity and New Technologies*

José Martiñán Soler | *The Strength of Color*

Kisho Kurokawa Architect & Associates | *Tradition and Modernity*

Mark Guard Architects | *Synthesis with Tradition*

MVRDV | *A House in the Netherlands*

Seth Stein Architects | *A House in Notting Hill*

Shigeru Ban | *Furniture Made to Measure*

Shoei Yoh + Architects | *The Dialogue with Nature*

Simon Conder | *The Warmth of Wood*

Ufficio di Architettura | *Sharing the Landscape, An Apartment by the Sea, An Organized and Welcoming Space, Art and History, An Apartment in Turin.*

Waro Kishi + K. Associates | *Imitating the Surroundings, A House in Kurakuen*

Xavière Bouyer | *Light in a Leading Role*

contents

introduction

minimalist rooms

"The light and textures of a space

This is how John Pawson, a British architect considered by many to be the master of minimalism, sums up two of the basic concepts of the movement: light and pure materials. To these two concepts we must add simplicity and a formal austerity that does not reveal the complexity of the construction techniques.

This movement began in the mid sixties as a form of aesthetics that was neither intended to be pictorial nor sculptural and which ended up being all of these things and more. Currently, minimalism is used in a more extended way and is also used as an adjective to define not only architectural elements, but also interiors such as those illustrated in this book.

The thirty-two projects that follow have some features in common that are characteristic of the minimalist movement. In addition, they are all large open spaces. To achieve this as many of the architectural barriers as possible have been eliminated and, often, the fundamental structure has been left exposed. What Ludwig Mies van der Rohe referred to as "the skeleton and skin" of a building is nothing more than this: structure and light.

can be a work of art."

Luminosity is another essential feature that is strengthened by the heavy use of the color white, monochromes, and large glazed areas. The windows not only improve the illumination, but they also become vehicles for communicating with the exterior environment with which enriching dialogues are established.

It was also Mies van der Rohe who defined the fundamental features of the minimalist environment in the following sentence: "If something does not serve for at least three things, then it does not serve at all." The elements used in the construction and the furniture tend to fulfill multiple functions. They generally act as area dividers, whether fixed or movable, in addition to being work surfaces or storage cupboards and, in this way, they maximize the amount of space available.

Minimalism does away with all that is irrelevant to emphasize what is important, and by doing so, results in liberty. In this respect, it has a lot in common with the way life is understood by non-consumer societies, in which the home is also a place for calmness and reflection, for resting and for peacefulness, and where the sacred coexists with everyday activity.

Imitating the Surroundings

Waro Kishi was the architect commissioned to design this house in Fukaya, near Tokyo. The design was influenced to a great extent by the location of the residence in the suburbs of the northern zone of Kanto, well known for its monotonous semi-urban landscape. Kishi's proposal consisted of a house closed off to its surroundings and open to its interior spaces.

The floor plan of the house is rectangular and has been distributed into three areas determined by function. The garage is located in the southern part and the bedrooms on the upper level. The north wing, raised half a level, accommodates the living room and the dining room with a ceiling more than thirteen feet in height. In the center of the building, a patio with an uncovered swimming pool visually links and also separates the other areas.

The patio constitutes an extension of the formal area, as it too can be a living and dining area. With the intention of minimizing the visual impact of the structure that divides the two areas, Kishi projected a series of metal posts, set independently of the wall, to which glass is fitted directly. The use of industrial materials responds to the architect's desire that the house should fit in with its surroundings and, at the same time, stamp a strong character on it by leaving all of the details of its structure exposed ∎

The structural elements have been intentionally left exposed by the architect in order to create an urban industrial atmosphere keeping with the surroundings in which the residence is located.

The interior patio, where the swimming pool is situated, links the private and formal zones. The use of glass and the way in which the same material used for the floor inside has been used to cover part of the ground outside, extends the area of the living and dining zone.

The staircase, in addition to being aesthetically pleasing, is cleverly positioned over the swimming pool, making the most of the available space.

The metal structure that supports the building is symmetrical. The artificial lighting creates a modern urban atmosphere.

The patio reflects the overall concept of the house—closed to the exterior, but open in the interior.

A view of the swimming pool can be enjoyed from the room on the upper level.

Adapting to the Surroundings

This detached house in Dorbirn, Austria, was designed by Baumschlager & Eberle, a studio that has a lot of experience with minimalist architecture. The architects in this team concentrate more on perfecting constructions of this type than on innovation. Each new project allows them, for this reason, to use their previously accumulated knowledge to go one step further.

For this residence, an orthogonal shape with strong lines was proposed. A second volume of an elongated form is anchored to the principal box and to the ridge of the slope which, in the way that it has been adapted to the landscape, permits a greater use of the available space as well as greater enjoyment of the natural surroundings. The asymmetry that has been produced between both blocks allows the noble spaces of the house to be differentiated.

Natural light floods into the interior due to the large enclosing glazed surfaces and to the elongated skylights spread out over the upper floor. White is used for the walls and ceilings which emphasize the luminosity and amplitude of the areas. For the flooring and furniture, wood was selected with the intention of creating a warm atmosphere. The design pursues comfort more than modern lines ■

minimalist pragmatism

The studio enjoys privileged views of the valley. The wood and fabrics used in the studio create a welcoming atmosphere.

On the next page, top, a detail of the staircase illuminated by sunlight from one of the elongated skylights.

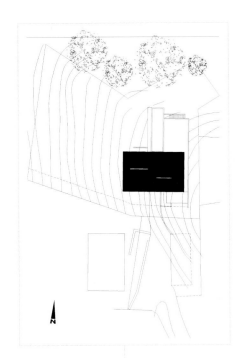

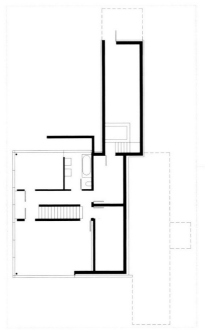

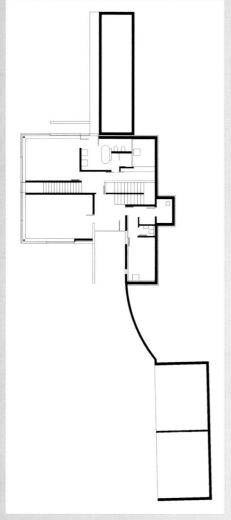

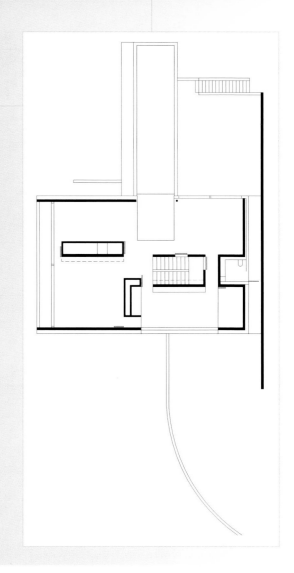

Above, the floor plan has been divided in the center by the staircase that connects the three levels and organizes the spaces.

On the following page, bottom, a cross-section of the building. The design of the different floors has been adapted to the landscape so as to obtain more usable space.

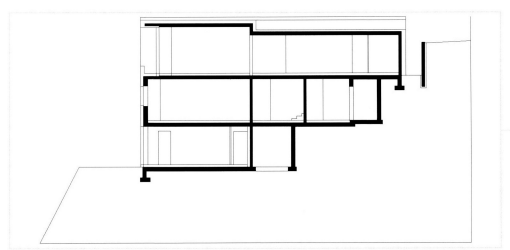

Simplification of Space

The refurbishing of this rooftop apartment situated in Clerkenwell, London, was complicated by the complexity of the original layout of the space, which had been constructed as a printing house in the thirties. Fortunately, this apparent difficulty turned out to be positive when it came to designing the residence.

The basic structure of the apartment allowed for the creation of a fluid series of innovative spaces, defined by function, volume, and location. The distribution is essentially open. Over the central area of the floor plan, a mezzanine has been constructed. A bedroom with a bathroom was situated in this zone of the residence. From this area, a terrace on the flat roof can be accessed. The double height of the principal living area is visually balanced by the more closed zones: the dining area and the kitchen.

With the intention of making the most of the natural light available, Form Design Architecture, the team of architects commissioned to design the project, designed one of the walls that separates the living area and the terrace as a glass and aluminum structure. This transparent wall has several doors through which the terrace can be accessed. The designs for all the windows on the north, east, and west facades were developed based on the premise of maximizing the illumination available from the outside ■

minimalist elegance

In the bedroom, the light has not only been strengthened by the predominate use of white in the furniture and accessories, but also by the design, which includes elongated windows over the low cupboards installed on the wall opposite the bed.

Geometric lines dominate the design of these spaces. A series of columns gives a restrained elegance to the living and dining area. The original curved profile of the ceiling has been accentuated due to beams of light that stem from the columns.

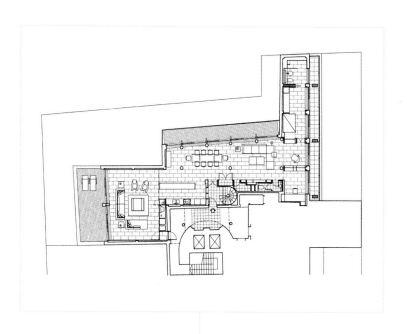

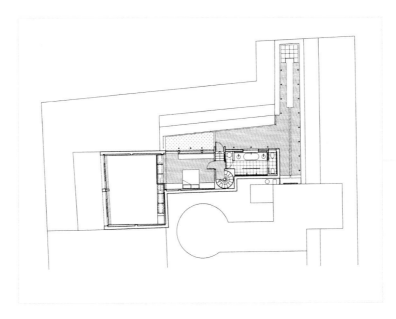

A House in Kurakuen

The location of this house in a residential area situated in the hills of Hashin, Japan, imposed certain conditions on the project. From its location, excellent panoramic views of the suburbs of the city of Osaka can be enjoyed. The inclination of the slope on which it is sited has a gradient of thirty degrees and is oriented towards the sea.

The first step that Waro Kishi, the architect commissioned to undertake the project, took was to establish the nature of the relationship that the house would have with such a striking landscape. The result consisted of two blocks with skeletons of reinforced steel. The one on the left accommodates the private zones while the one on the right accomodates the public zones including the living area and the kitchen. The two blocks are connected via a ramp.

On the upper floor, a bedroom with terrace is located. The large horizontal windows seem to extend toward the exterior due to the absence of frames around them. This feature is found in all of the bedrooms which, against all expectations, are the areas most open to the exterior, while in the public zones the windows are smaller in size ■

ntality

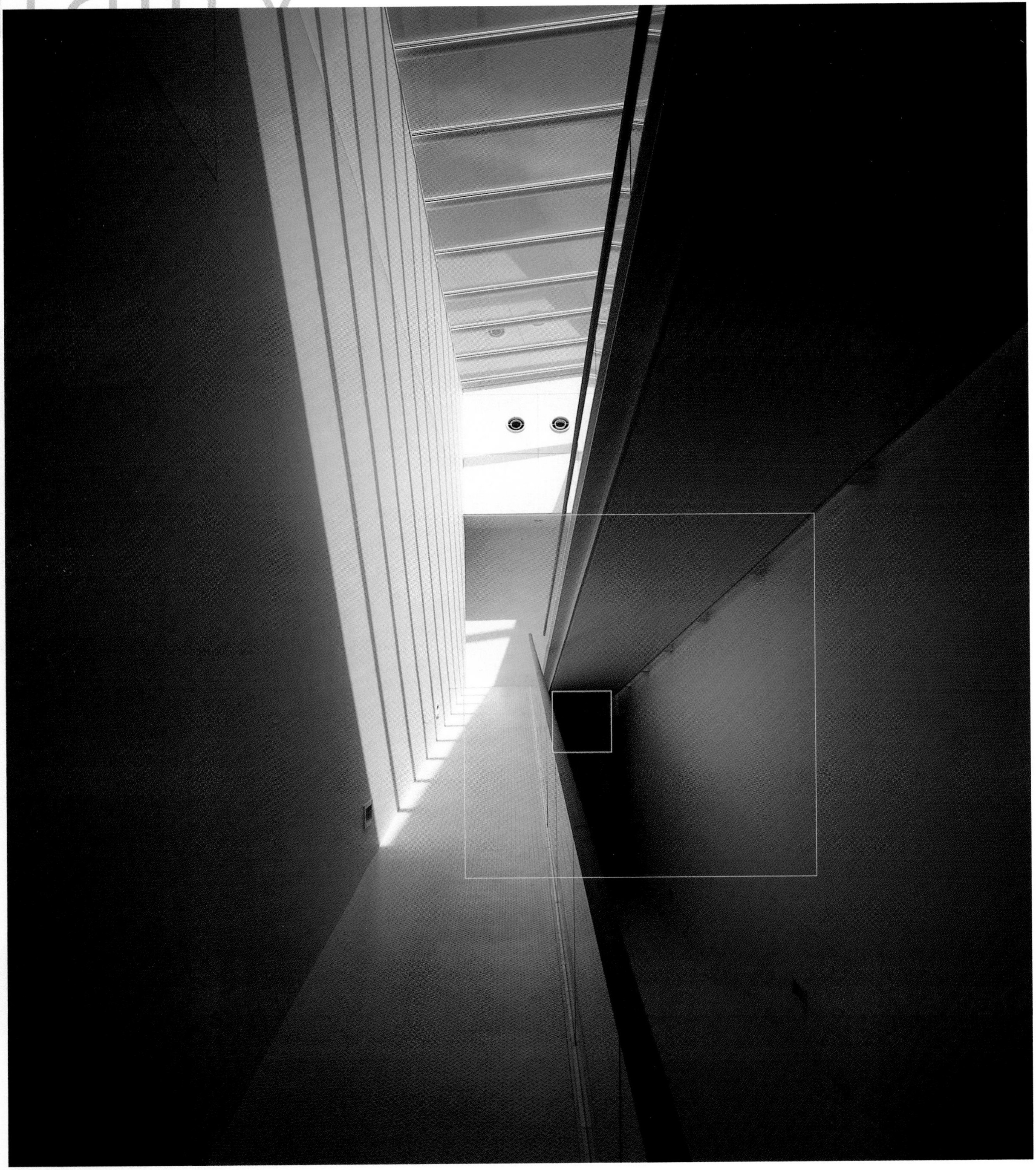

Above, the bedroom on the upper floor opens up to the landscape and adjoining terrace. The views from the bedrooms have been highlighted due to the marked horizontality of the windows.

The kitchen island stands out for its simple lines and for the absence of decorative elements.

The bathroom opens onto a small enclosed patio, but the privacy has been preserved. The exterior space is presented as an extension of the interior.

Art and History

This house, located in the center of Turin, was remodeled according to the directives of the residents, a young couple and their daughter. A team of architects of Ufficio di Architettura undertook the project, in which changes to the existing walls were to be minimal. An epoxy flooring system was installed and the walls and window frames have been treated in a similar color to the one used on the floor to attain a homogeneous whole.

When it came to laying out the spaces, the Japanese philosophy of dedicating some areas to the contemplation of works of art was followed. Another unusual feature of this home is a series of stratified glass panels that serve as spatial dividers and as screens on which to project slides. As requested by the clients, some of the areas have been left empty to allow the aesthetics of the artworks or images, in many cases family keepsakes, to stand out.

The residence is clearly characterized by the aesthetics of a traditional Japanese house. It has been almost completely divested of objects, in such a way that the emotional impact of the decorative elements selected is much stronger. The artwork has acquired a strong architectural spirit in as much as they go far beyond their function of being a separating element to become a vehicle for dialogue between physical and virtual spaces ■

The minimalist influence contrasts with the explosion of form and color in the artwork. Very large pieces are exhibited and provide a vehicle for dialogue between physical and virtual spaces.

The scarcity of decorative objects gives special importance to the elements selected.

The predominance of straight lines in the residence, and the austerity in decoration, create an ordered atmosphere.

Natural light floods this corridor from various sources. The shelving and the grain in the wood that covers the floor emphasize the horizontality of the house.

A Gallery Viewpoint

The Gallery MA is situated in a hilly area between the sea and mountains in the national park of Genkai, two hours from the city of Fukuoka. The main objective of the project was to site the building on a steeply sloping hilltop fifty-six feet higher than the surrounding land. The solution consisted of a building formed by five volumes, one set over the other. The space was destined to be an exhibition area and workshop for a visual artist. Therefore, functionality and good light were the central concerns when it came to developing the project.

White walls and clean-lined spaces give the interior of the gallery a feeling of purity and fluidity from one area to another. The materials used in the construction, including cement, cedar wood, pleated polycarbonate, steel plate, and metal mesh stamp a modern and functional feeling on the building.

It was fundamental to optimize the amount of natural light flowing in in order to illuminate the artist's exhibition area. It was intended to be a multi-use space, given that the upper level was destined to be a concert area. Large openings in the structure of the facade, from which the view can be seen, allow light to penetrate into the building free from obstruction and to transmit a spiritual ambience. A glazed showcase allows light through to the lower levels and creates a relationship between the different floors.

The workshop where the artist works was designed as a space independent from the rest of the building so that it would have greater privacy ■

nplation

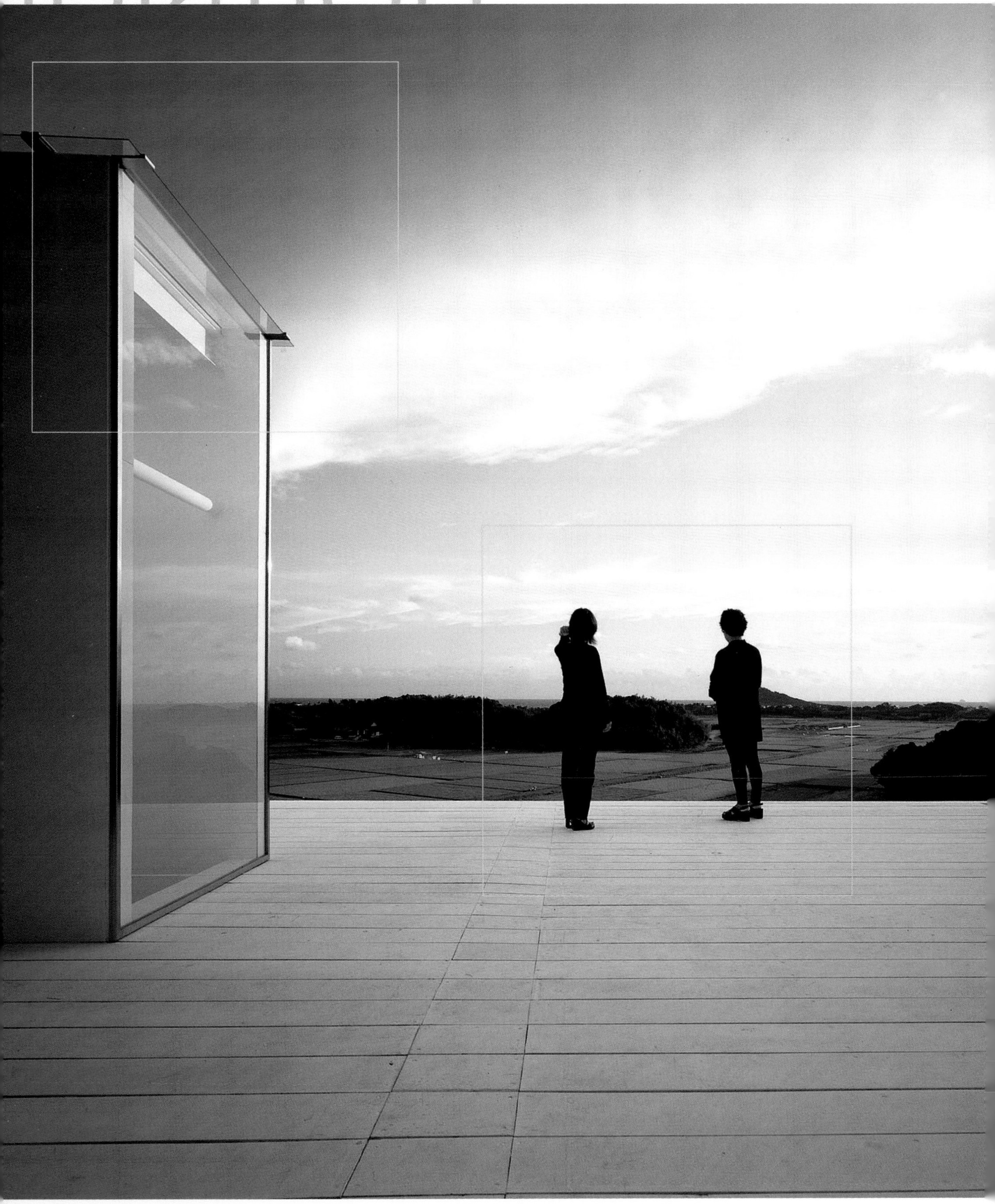

minimalist contemplation

This area, dedicated to exhibiting the works of the artist, offers a privileged view of lake Genka-nada and its surroundings. The combination of the contemplation of the exterior landscape, through the various openings, with that of the artwork inside creates an atmosphere of perfect serenity for the gallery.

The artworks are exhibited on the glazed surfaces to make the most of the available natural light. The lower floor, in turn, receives light emitting from this privileged area.

Light in a Leading Role

In this duplex apartment located in a neighborhood of Paris that is well know for its traffic and nightlife, there were two main objectives when it came to remodeling: to make the most of the natural light available and to maintain privacy.

During the transformation of the apartment, the intention was to make the most of the available space. All sorts of unnecessary architectural barriers were eliminated to create open spaces and to facilitate the entrance of natural light into all areas of the residence. This is a fundamental aspect in a city in which the weather is far from merciful.

Light has become the major feature of this space and forms an enveloping skin around the interior of the home in which the color white predominates. Its impact brings out the textures of the different materials, such as polished and painted concrete for the floor and cedar wood, treated for the bathroom or finished in white for the kitchen.

A large open space containing different areas defined by their distribution over the two floors and by the location of furniture, along with curtains in the same color, allow for a degree of privacy to be obtained without shutting off light to other areas. On the upper floor, good use has been made of natural light thanks to a glazed roof in which a simple system of metal rails has been incorporated to prevent the bedroom from being on view from the outside ■

minimalist intimacy

The staircase, situated in one extreme of the rest area, connects the two floors and additionally fulfills the function of a bookcase. Both levels have been conceived as individual open spaces in which curtains separate the different zones according to function.

The kitchen has been fitted out with furniture with restrained lines. Some decorative elements and certain aesthetic details add a touch of color that contrasts with the overall whiteness.

A Duplex Apartment with Views of Downtown

This project consisted of unifying two attics with a terrace located in a Manhattan building of historical interest. The studio Gabelli Associates was commissioned to design the interior space, which enjoys outstanding views of downtown New York.

The backbone of the two volumes is the white marble spiral staircase, which is the central axis of the residence. It was conceived as a floating ribbon that connects the living room with the bedroom on the lower floor, and which is made up of a cascade of marble platforms united by an axis similar to a spine.

The same material has been used to cover the floor and thus a great luminosity emanates throughout the space. Austerity dominates the rooms, in the spirit of of the essence of the project: to strengthen the light, simplicity and the textures of a linear space.

Visually, all of the elements emphasize the verticality of the structure, which is reinforced by the height of the ceilings, giving the interior of the residence magnitude and serenity. The austerity highlights the modern design and the pure lines of the furniture.

The predominating natural illumination has been enhanced by the range of light colors used in the space. Thanks to the straightness of the angles, shadows of any type that could upset the transparency of the ambience have been avoided ∎

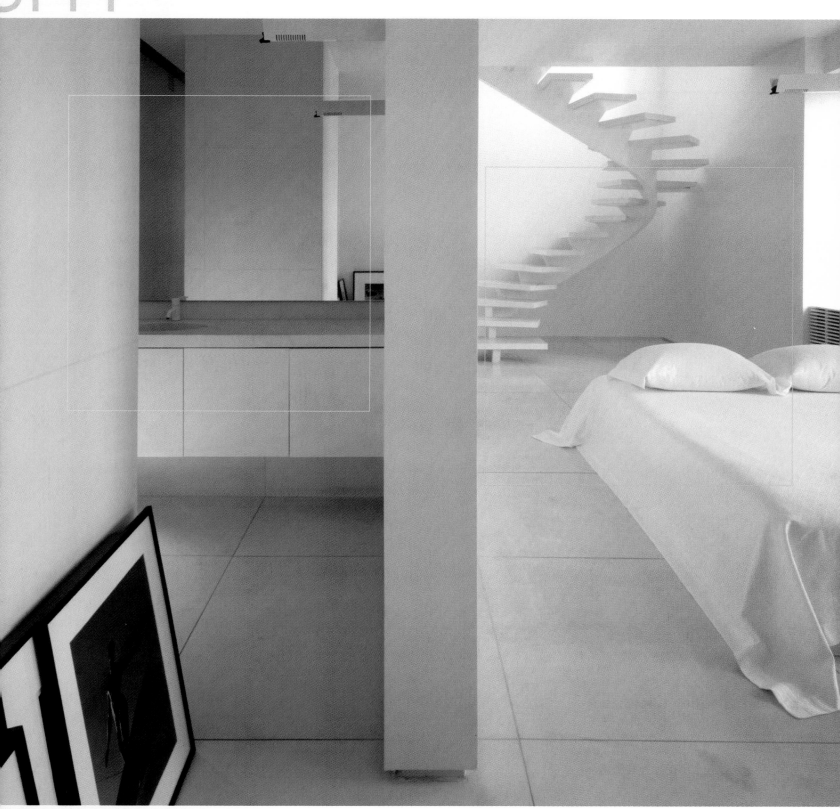

The decorative elements are minimal. However, they have been perfectly selected. In the living/dining room the decorative elements have been reduced to a minimum in order to create a restrained ambience that transmits tranquility. The furniture reflects the different ambiences.

Conceptual Spaces

This rooftop apartment, situated in A Coruña, Spain, has been renovated by A-Cero Arquitectos. The project pursued two major objectives: to eliminate unnecessary walls and to obtain more natural light. The great expressiveness obtained by the use of color and volume, which are reminiscent of compositions from abstract expressionism, stands out.

The original apartment was a dark space divided into a number of small compartments. The first stage of refurbishing consisted of demolishing the partition walls to bring natural light into corners of the apartment. The sensation of spaciousness has been enhanced due to the use of built-in wardrobes and the generous use of white paint.

The intermediary floor, which accommodates the bedroom, dressing room, and bathroom, remains visually isolated from the rest of the apartment due to an opaque glass balustrade. The pillar that supported this mezzanine has been replaced by a brace anchored in the ceiling.

The illumination has been designed with great care. Warm- and cold-colored sources of light, which can be used to modify the ambience as desired, have been carefully combined. The design of some of the pieces of furniture, and the decorative details such as the colors of the lights, imbue the space with a futuristic air ■

minimalist abstraction

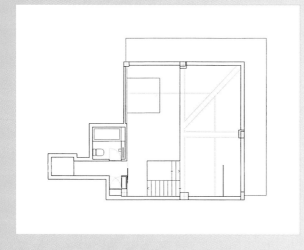

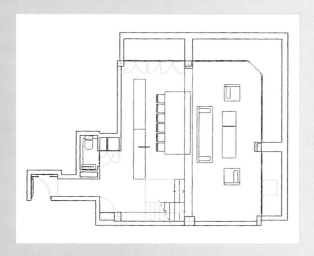

All of the furniture was custom made as part of the project. All of the decorative details, from the picture frames to the sofas, have been selected carefully. The kitchen fittings stand out for their complexity.

The staircase, with its cantilevered steps that appear to float in space, links the formal zone with the rest area. The play on color and volume gives a great visual presence to this element, which forms part of the dark green and white composition in the living room.

minimalist abstraction

Above, the kitchen opens into the living/dining room. The worktop serves to separate the two areas.

The bedroom furniture has a Japanese influence. A large work of art catches attention in this space, in which there is a pronounced contrast between black and white.

Light and austerity predominate. The atmosphere is imbued with serenity.

The Outside as an Extension of the Inside

The design of this apartment highlights the surrounding seascape. This is not surprising, given that the apartment is situated on the water's edge and enjoys spectacular views of the Bahia de Palma. The architect's goal was to integrate the exterior into the interior of the residence. This idea has been reinforced by the use of traditional building materials found locally, such as natural limestone, along with natural white fabrics.

The first stage of the refurbishing consisted of unifying two properties into one apartment. The space is organized around an open area that comprises a living zone, dining zone, and kitchen. The furniture extends more horizontally than vertically, and the individual pieces are low and allow for the creation of spatial divisions that do not form barriers.

The large windows in the living area and the two terraces that form part of the residence offer a continual dialogue with the environment. A long counter, thirty-nine feet in length, constructed in natural limestone, functions not only as a table for the dining area and for one of the terraces, but also as a work surface in the kitchen, creating a means of communication with the exterior ■

The natural light, along with the use of white, are the outstanding features of this space. The color of the wood is reminiscent of the sand on the beaches on the other side of the large windows.

Austerity and simplicity define the atmosphere of this residence. The decorative elements have been kept to a minimum, and as with the ceramic work, show a marked influence of local materials.

The Dialogue with Nature

With this house, located in Nagasaki-shi, Japan, Shoei Yoh initiated his investigations into buildings with "environmental systems" that establish a dialogue with nature. This concept is manifested as much in the exterior of the residence as in the interior, in which the geometric network structure is repeated.

The essence of this project was to achieve a volume by means of light. In the joints of the panels that make up the building, a fine glazed band has been inserted which permits beams of light to enter the house during the day while at night, artificial light is projected to the outside.

The same checkered pattern is reproduced in the furniture, in the accessories, and in the materials used for the walls and floors. An articulated space contained within a symmetrical structure has been created and is only broken by a four-stepped staircase that crosses the construction diagonally and which is extended into the exterior area of the building.

The floor plan of the house has been distributed into two clearly differentiated zones. An intermediate space full of light, situated between the two symmetrical volumes and closed off by transparent glass, acts as a divider for these two areas, one for private use and the other for public use ■

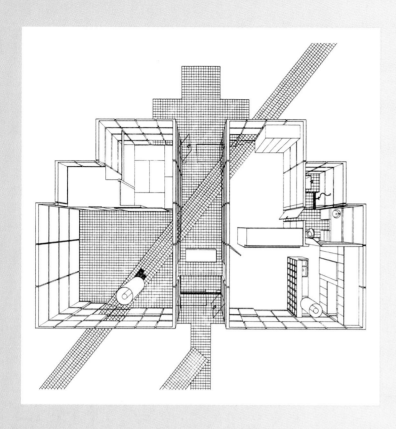

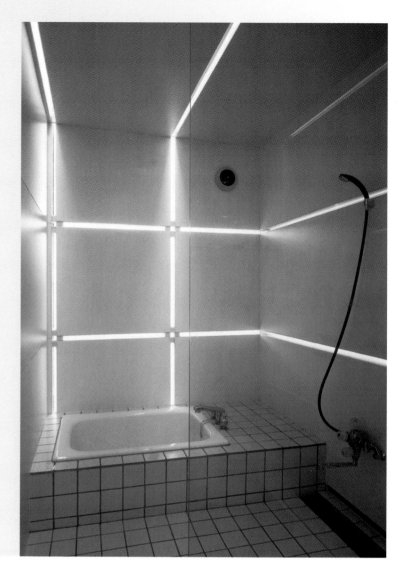

In the bathroom, the exterior network has been reproduced as much as in the floor as in the walls. Even a shower base that reproduces the same pattern has been selected. The whiteness of the beams of light creates an atmosphere of serenity and mysticism.

On the right, a white screen separates the different zones without breaking the spatial unity.

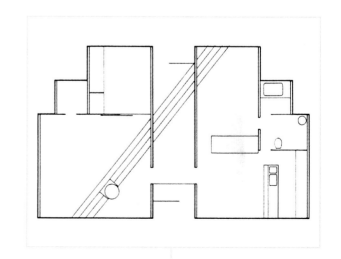

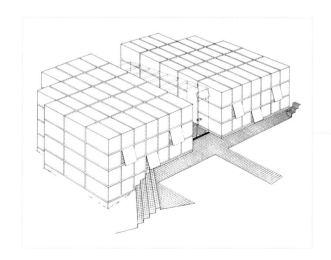

A Workshop Made Into a Home

This residence is located in a central district of Barcelona known as the Eixample. A team of architects formed by Joan Llongueras, Jaume Alba, and Jordi Mercè were commissioned to undertake the refurbishing, which basically consisted of doing away with all of the partitions and creating an open space that would be comfortable and visually spacious.

Given the impossibility of carrying out structural modifications to the supporting walls of this old workshop, located on the ground floor of the building, the architects decided to excavate into the floor and create a small mezzanine. Due to this measure, not only has the usable surface area of the residence been increased, but there has also been a noticeable increase in the amount of natural light entering the area.

An auxiliary building in the interior patio, which accommodates a small garden, has given the kitchen natural light. This latter space is connected to the dining room. A large piece of wooden furniture hides the bedroom that is situated in the area between the floors. This piece of furnishing creates a pleasing visual impact in the residence. Its design incorporates compartments for storing clothes or utensils. ∎

The sycamore floor, the white of the walls, and the use of indirect lighting combine to create a serene atmosphere. A gray wall separates the studio from the dining and living areas.

The furniture and worktop, which define the studio, have been made in the same material as the floor to give a sensation of homogeneity. In the bedroom, on the right, a large wardrobe in dark wood stands out.

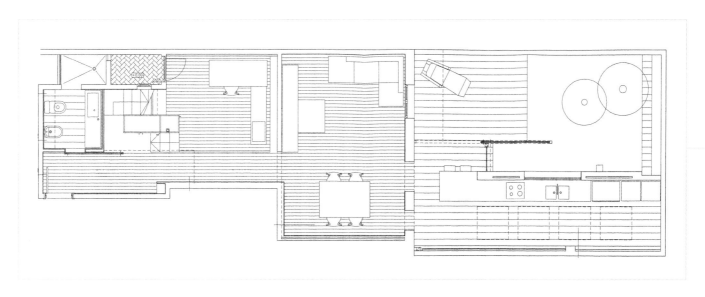

The Fluidity of Space

This project puts a special emphasis on the distribution of each of the spaces in these offices. With the intention of making the most of the available space, barriers have been eliminated and separating modules installed to differentiate the departments.

The contrast between the colored elements and the immaculate white walls give the space a great expressiveness. The colors are daring and free-and-easy and manage to create an ambience that is modern and informal. These elements, in addition, fulfill the function of defining the different areas.

Thanks to the precision with which the office furniture and decorative accessories have been selected, and to the successful way in which they have been positioned within the white structure, an air of order and serenity is found, which contrasts with the chaotic movement generated by the activity in the workplace.

The large windows in the facade guarantee the entrance of the natural light that fills the space with vitality and emphasizes the strength of the colored elements. The artificial illumination again strengthens this effect with lamps that hang from the ceiling and illuminate work zones along with other sources of light, some of which are projected vertically and others horizontally ■

A completely transparent glass panel delimits a meeting room, and the autonomy of the area is maintained without disturbing the unity of the space.

The furniture, cupboards, and shelves fulfill the function of not only separating the different zones, but also of minimizing visual obstruction to facilitate the fluidity of the space.

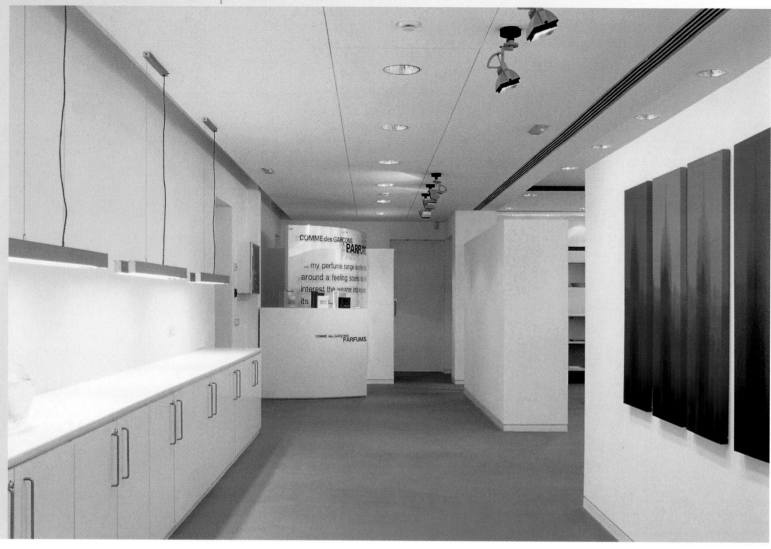

The small display case and transparent semi-cylindrical panel illuminated by a red light generates a visually eye-catching contrast and creates an informal atmosphere.

The storage cupboards are integrated into the structure, and due to their color they are assimilated into the setting and help create an atmosphere that is conducive to communication.

Coexistence Between the Past
and the Present

This apartment is located in a building in Stockholm that enjoys excellent views of the city's port and has access to an adjacent garden. The client, a teacher of economics, owns two of the floors in this neoclassical building in which he has taken up residence.

The refurbishing work consisted of maintaining the original windows and floors and eliminating the interior walls that had been constructed over the years. A staircase, located in a small, intricately designed space, connects the two levels of the living area.

Both the furniture used in this space and the floor are constructed of oak. The two elements combine in such a way that there is no loss of simplicity. Their pure lines of rectilinear finishes characterize the furnishings.

On the upper floor, a new bathroom has been designed, from which the views of the port can be enjoyed from within a relaxing and spiritual atmosphere. The garden table, which was conceived as a permanent element, has been constructed on site ■

The wood that has been used in the kitchen is oak, and is used elsewhere in the apartment. Simplicity and pure straight lines characterize the design.

The colors of the steps alternate, keeping with the intricate design of the staircase.

The walls, which were constructed over the years, have been eliminated in order to create a sensation of spaciousness. The windows and floors have been preserved and restored. This mixture of the new and the old leads to an enriching overall effect.

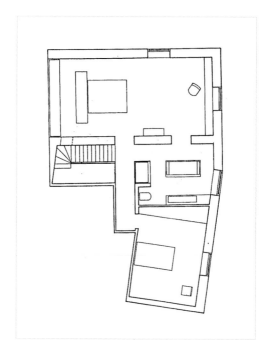

Furniture Made to Measure

The design of this house, for which Shigeru Ban is responsible, has been based on respect for the house's natural surroundings. The building is situated in the mountains of Yamanaka in the middle of a dense landscape of high fir trees which contrast with the horizontal nature of the residence, which itself seems to wish to go unnoticed.

With the intention of easing the construction process, prefabricated units, which guaranteed quality control over the project and considerably reduced the costs, were used. In addition to these virtues, the prefabricated units determined the dimensions of the project and act as structural and spatial dividers of the different areas.

The eight-foot-high pieces vary in width according to the use for which they are intended. These dimensions oscillate between three feet for storage wardrobes and one-and-a-half feet for bookcases and shelves. Visually, the interior space is a homogenized whole due to the use of the color white. In this almost monochromatic environment, the large windows and the exterior landscape stand out ∎

eneity

The furniture fulfills the function of separating the areas as if they were walls. Reduced to a minimum, these divisions create clear luminous spaces.

During the day, the large windows allow the residence to be flooded with light while at night, the house illuminates its immediate surroundings.

Cubists Structures

During the refurbishing of this residence in Alenquer, a town in Portugal to the north of Lisbon, the exterior walls, of great architectural value, were uncovered. These structures stamp a strong character on the spaces.

The design of this project, undertaken by architects from the Aires Mateus & Asociados studio, was as concerned about the exterior spaces as the interior ones. The result is an intricate distribution of great visual impact. The play between the light and shade projected by the different volumes and the different volumes themselves reflects the influence of cubism.

One of the goals for this remodeling was to create spaces that are light and open. To achieve this, glass roofing, which contrasts with the consistency of the walls of great thickness, was used. The interior floor, along with part of the ground outside, has been covered with wood. This created a sensation of continuity and fluidity as well as an atmosphere of warmth.

One of the particularities of this residence lies in the swimming pool, which is delimited by the walls of the building on one side, but uncovered on the other. This is reminiscent of oriental baths ■

The contrast between tradition and the avant-garde reaches a high level in this residence.

An intimate atmosphere is achieved due to the structure of the building.

The intricacy of the volumes in the house is reminiscent of the cubist style. This feature is reinforced by the play of light and shade.

The idea of using white for the walls and light-colored wood for the floor inside and for the ground outside visually balances the space with its simplicity.

A wall with a number of perforations, situated between the swimming pool and the garden, separates both spaces and preserves a certain amount of privacy.

The artificial lighting contrasts with the darkness of the other areas and gives a dreamy air to this space.

An Organized and Welcoming Space

The owners of this duplex apartment in Turin, a young couple dedicated to the automotive industry and fashion design, placed particular emphasis on achieving an extremely organized space in order to optimize the space of the apartment.

The project was part of an overall refurbishing of the eighteenth-century building in which it is located. The work also affected a wooden ceiling and part of a structural brick wall that has been replaced by a structure of metal and laminated glass, by which both floors have gained natural light.

Next to the entrance door, a large bookcase occupies the entire wall from the lowest level to the ceiling and, to a large extent, frees the rest of the residence from furniture. The staircase that connects the two floors is almost unnoticeable because it stands next to a piece of furniture and is of a construction based on cantilevered steps without a handrail. The overall impression of lightness is completed with the use of glass in the last part of the entryway. This is intended to provide the illumination to the lower floor.

On the first floor, a storeroom and two bedrooms with bathrooms have been located, in addition to the entryway, while upstairs an open space defined by the furnishings and the staircase accommodates the kitchen and the living/dining area ■

Visually, the staircase seems to form part of the bookcase. The combination of the different types of wood in the flooring and stairs, along with successfully engineered lighting, creates a harmonious and welcoming atmosphere.

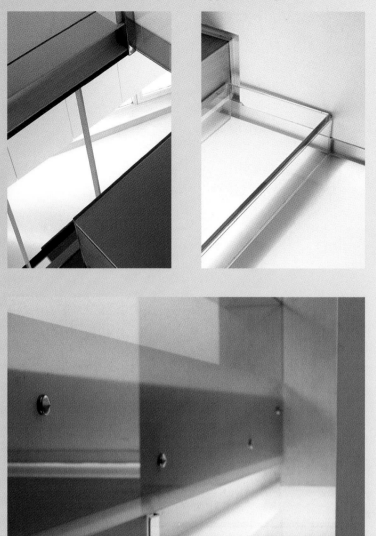

Above, a detail of the staircase that connects the two floors. The last section of the staircase is constructed of glass, in order to let light through.

Restrained lines and warm tones predominate in the bathroom. A large mirror makes the area appear noticeably more spacious.

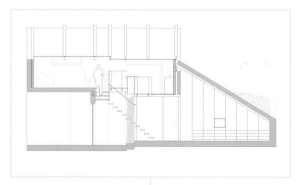

The Warmth of Wood

The journalist Annalisa Barbieri and the photographer Pete Warren are the owners of this residence situated on the second floor of a converted nineteenth-century warehouse in London. As the initial idea was to maintain the openness of the original space, the architects designed a module to accommodate the kitchen and bathroom and to avoid the necessity of putting up partition walls. The overall design offers a sensation of warmth achieved by the use of wood, which covers the floors and walls, and by the way the artificial lighting has been installed.

The area has been divided into three spaces, separated from each other by movable elements which fulfill the function of separating the different areas and strengthening their functionality without losing spatial unity. The separating elements were also designed to fulfill the function of furniture. They act as storage areas for clothes and books to supplement the built-in wardrobes in the service area.

The wooden cubicle that accommodates the kitchen and bathroom is slightly raised from the floor so that better views of the living area and out the windows can be enjoyed. An opening at the height of the kitchen worktop allows it to be used in two ways, either as a working area or as a serving counter. For the design of the bathroom, a system of doors has been created to allow the toilet, washbasin, and bathtub areas to be isolated as needed ■

The toilet, bathtub and washbasin have been designed with a system of doors that allows them to be used independently. The kitchen has been slightly raised from the floor and the gap created between the floor and the kitchen area has been used to locate a part of the lighting system. This creates a very special urban atmosphere.

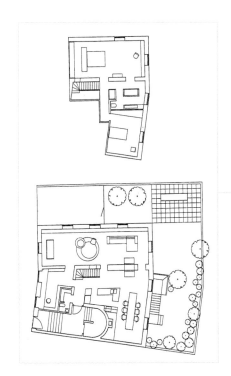

Rocks from the Desert

The objective of this project, located in Stockholm, was to renovate an apartment with an attic and to convert it into a living space for one of the architects who was working on the team that was undertaking the project. The team converted the old attic into a useful area by creating a small terrace off of it. They designed the lower floor as a continuous open space in which the only area with a door is the bathroom.

In the apartment, the spaces are distributed according to their use: public or private. The bedroom and study are situated on the upper floor so as to enjoy greater privacy while the entrance, dining room, kitchen, and living room have been located on the floor below.

A staircase, hidden behind a wall between the dining room and kitchen, connects the two levels. The steps are suspended in the air and there is no protective handrail.

What especially stands out about this project is the contrast of color, the textures of the various surfaces that result from the use of materials such as rock from the Arizona desert, and the whiteness of the walls and ceilings. This chromatic interplay imbues the atmosphere with the peace and serenity that was desired by the owner.

Furnishing has been reduced to the indispensable, and it has been selected following neutral forms so as to give priority to the space. The intention was to accentuate the light in such a manner as to reflect the whiteness of the structure and reinforce the initial idea of continuous space and restraint ■

The lower floor has been organized as a continuous space in which the only area with a door is the bathroom. The areas have been designed according to their use: public or private.

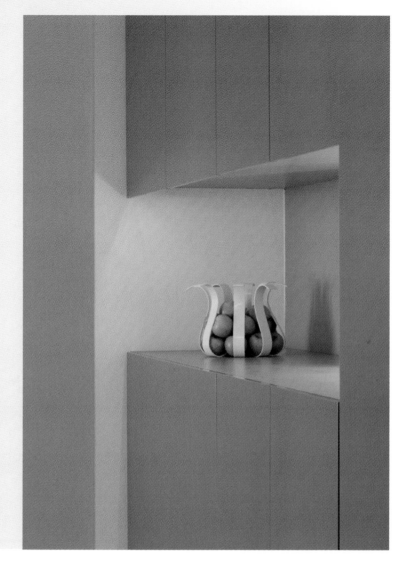

The furniture, with its restrained lines and warm colors, along with the materials used on certain surfaces, contrasts with the white paint, visually enriching the whole with different textures.

An Apartment in Turin

This apartment occupies the first floor of a three-story building constructed in the fifties. The property also includes a garden situated at the back of the apartment block. The renovation of the apartment was undertaken bearing in mind the necessity of including a couple of bedrooms with bathrooms and a dressing room. The architects of Ufficio di Architettura worked with warm materials to create a welcoming atmosphere as asked for by the client, a young bank manager.

Wood was the material chosen for the floors and furniture to create a warm and relaxing atmosphere. Some of the main pieces of furniture have been made in laminated palisander (rosewood), while the kitchen utensils are hidden behind white wooden walls which run from floor to ceiling to give the feeling of spaciousness. All of the wooden surfaces have been treated with oil to give them a natural look.

The space is distributed into two independent areas, each with its own bathroom. Sliding panels of translucent glass reaching from floor to ceiling and framed in light steel let the natural light into even the darkest corners during the day ■

In the dining room, some of the furniture seems to disappear into the walls. This effect has been achieved by painting some of the wooden panels that reach from floor to ceiling white.

The accessories follow the overall trend in residential decoration: simplicity.

The use of wood, which extends to the bathroom, creates a soothing atmosphere.

Opposite, a detail of the translucent glass doors that reach from floor to ceiling in their light steel frames. Their function is to let the light in during the day, and during the night, to filter the artificial illumination.

Classic Purity and New Technologies

The Johnson Chou studio directed the refurbishing of this residence located in Toronto. The project consisted of eliminating all of the nonstructural walls and creating an orderly space inspired by the characteristics of a prison. The plans called for new geometric volumes and the application of the new technologies. Sliding sandblasted glass panels separate the different areas.

The team of architects worked with basic materials such as aluminum and concrete that offer a classic purity reaffirmed by the absence of secondary elements. The storage areas are located within this backdrop as an extension of the walls. The complete area has been intelligently illuminated with fluorescent and halogen lamps.

The essential concept of the project, a structural order, is manifested in the master bedroom and the bathrooms through the design and materials used, such as dark metals, which are most suitable to recreate a cold atmosphere that is orderly. The bathroom is situated over a platform of slate and is completely surrounded by transparent glass walls, which allows this zone to be observed from all places within the apartment ■

minimalist classicism

On the right, the bed does not rest on the floor but is fitted to the wall by its aluminum structure which gives it the appearance of being firm and robust.

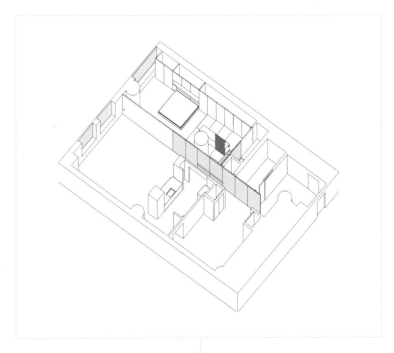

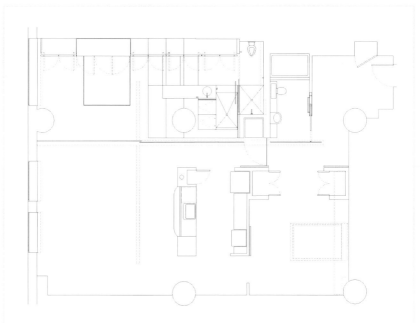

A glazed screen surrounds the bath area, which is situated on a slate platform and which accommodates an large bathtub. The area has been conceived with the idea of creating an especially relaxing atmosphere.

Sharing the Landscape

This project, undertaken by various professionals of the Ufficio Di Architettura in collaboration with D. Volpe, consisted of expanding the living area of a rural house. Its location in Vandorno, Italy, on the slopes of the Alps guaranteed some spectacular views that were treated by the Japanese technique of *shakkei*, or "integrating the landscape." The scenes have been conceived of as an intellectual product which stems from the architecture and takes the form of pictures framed by the windows. They reach their height in the west-facing "viewpoint."

Additional square footage was added to the original surface area over two floors. On the first floor, the kitchen, bathroom, dining room, and one bedroom have been located, and on the second, another bedroom, a living area and a terrace. The new spaces have been conceived of as a series of filters which gradually lead from the closed interiors of the original building to the areas open to the natural environment. This has been achieved by adopting an architectural design based on the assembly of vertical and horizontal planes. As an echo of the traditional style, a structure of laminated wooden bands that are open towards the outside has been installed which frames the extension of the residence ■

The window becomes a picture in the tradition of the Japanese technique of *shakkei,* or integrating the landscape into the architecture, establishing a relationship between nature and culture.

The furniture has been carefully selected. The chairs in the dining room stand out for their avant-garde design.

Above, on the upper floor, a terrace and a balcony constructed in the traditional style of structures open to their surroundings.

The structure of wooden strips emphasizes reconciling space between inside and outside.

Sandstone paving, glass and aluminum roofing, plywood, and concrete surfaces have been used in the new construction.

Tradition and Modernity

This house, clearly influenced by Japanese design, is located in one of the most well-known neighborhoods of Tokyo. It is sited on a plot of land that is surrounded on all sides by a red-granite wall. A large extension of the surface area has allowed different zones to be developed. As a result, the residence consists of three different areas: the principal residence, the area dedicated to the tea ceremony, and the communicating bridge.

The design for this project, undertaken by Kisho Kurokawa Architect & Associates, fulfills all of the requirements to be considered pure minimalism. The bedrooms, distributed over three floors, stand out for the complete absence of furniture, which creates ideal conditions for reflection and serenity. A system of sliding doors allows the areas to be modified as desired.

The tea ceremony area consists of a small pavilion which, in its interior, contains a wooden structure that allows in light and, as a result, allows the views of the garden to be manipulated. This cubicle is surrounded by passages and by a gallery of paintings by the artist Hiroshi Senju. The transparent screens also make it possible to for the artwork to be contemplated from within the central room ■

Although the Japanese tradition is evident in the pavilion dedicated to the tea ceremony, a perfect balance with more present-day elements has also been obtained.

Four paintings from the series Water Fall, by the artist Hiroshi Senju, surround the area.

The windows, notably horizontal, are located near the floor, which strengthens privacy without hindering the entrance of natural light.

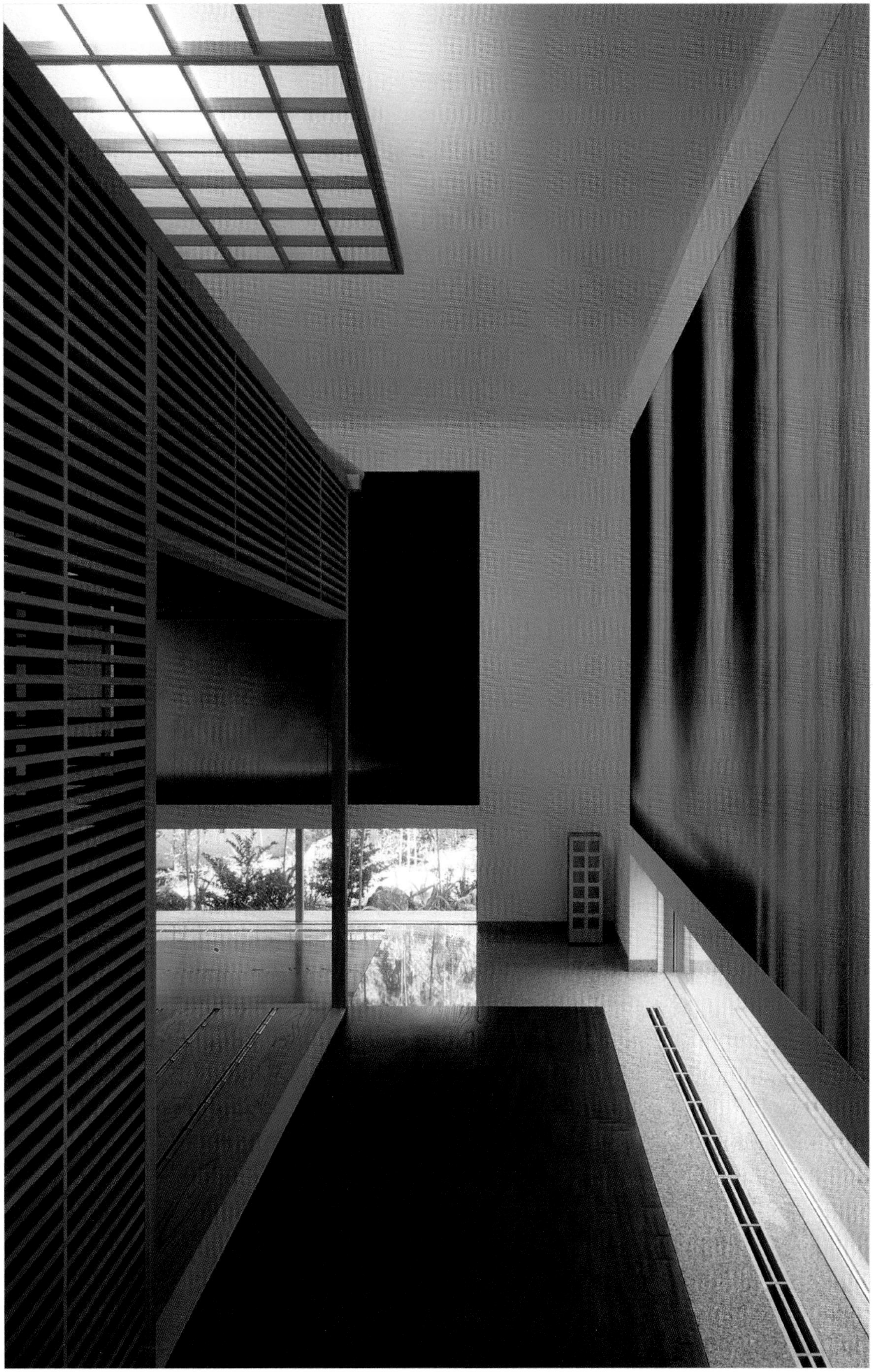

The elegant design of the walls maximizes the illumination of the interior spaces.

Above, the spiral staircase, which connects the different levels, takes on a strong scenic presence. It also creates an effect of rising fluidity.

The Strength of Color

The morphology of the land on which this house is situated was a determining factor in the design of the project. This residence is located in Mera, on the northwest coast of Spain, on a site with views of the city and the estuary of A Coruña.

The plot has been organized into terraces defined by green quartzite walls that follow the existent unevenness of the land. In these areas, different spaces are created due to elements such as porches, terraces, or pergolas.

One of the peculiarities of the project is the use of a great variety and richness of pavement. In the southern zone, alongside a number of exterior structures, a swimming pool has been located. An annex, which fulfills an organizational function, contains the dressing rooms and garage.

The residence was built on the highest point of the plot. It consists of three floors, two of which rise above ground level with the third partially dug into the earth. In the design of the different spaces, it was decided to feature the sea in such a way that it would become part of the home, but always from a different point of view ■

To dress the floors, walls, doors, and furniture, different types of visually enriching woods have been used which give the space great expressiveness.

The spectacular views of the Galician estuary form a fully integrated part of the different areas.

An interesting set of sliding doors allows for spaces to be opened or closed as needed.

The use of different types of wood and of other natural materials, such as stone, creates a warm atmosphere.

Volumetric Geometry

The refurbishing of this small twenty-year-old apartment block, situated in Fukuoaka, was based on the idea of reconciling the building with two important elements: the first, the steep slope on which the building had been constructed, and the second, an elevated highway that flanks the buiding. In Hiroyuki Arima's project, the access to the house was situated on the south side, where the highway passes by.

A decision was made to maintain the exterior structure and convert the interior space into a duplex apartment. The interior walls were eliminated to create an open space in which straight lines and geometric forms would dominate. The predominant use of the color white makes up for the scarcity of natural light coming into the building due to its northern orientation.

On the lower floor, in the hall to the apartment, three movable wooden boards which have a great presence and which contrast with the immaculate atmosphere have been installed. A handrail-free staircase, which seems to float, connects this floor with the upper level where some of the bedrooms are found. The light in these areas is filtered by translucent panels that manage to create a mystical atmosphere ■

The separation between the steps and the absence of a handrail gives the staircase a greater sensation of verticality.

In the bedrooms, the semitransparent panels allow for a play on light and shade that imbues delicacy and subtlety into the atmosphere and leaves to the imagination what could be found behind them, be it a landscape or another room.

On the right, a completely opaque black panel, installed as a divider between different areas, contrasts with the immaculate walls. The borders have no point of contact with the walls, which allows light from the upper and lower floors to shine through and frame the panel, placing even more emphasis on the contrast between light and dark.

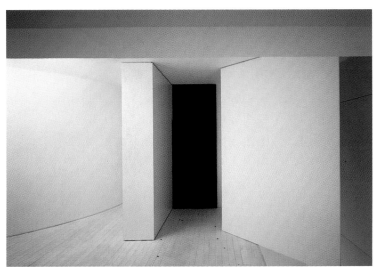

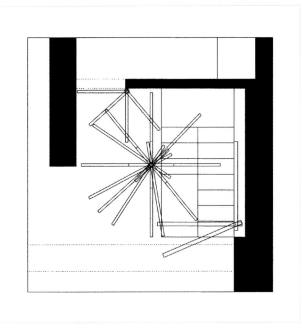

An Apartment by the Sea

The team of architects Uda (Ufficio di Architettura) were inspired by the interiors of boats when it came to remodeling this summer residence situated in Nice. The apartment is in a building from the fifties with spectacular views of the sea, which have been incorporated into the design and into the location of the building's openings.

A long narrow space and an annexed studio are what were available at the beginning of the project. One of the main objectives was to eliminate the walls of the different rooms to create one large space in which to concentrate the basic functions of the home.

The architects responsible for developing the project designed a system of sliding doors in transparent glass which modify the distribution of the living room and define the studio. This last area can also be converted into a guest room with its own bathroom and kitchen.

In the rest areas, the furniture blends into the space due to the white finishes and smooth surfaces, creating a calm and relaxing atmosphere. The lighting— in yellow, bluish or white—has been incorporated into the architectural structure and also emerges from the joints where the walls meet the ceiling as well as from some of the furniture ■

Above, in the bedroom, the whiteness of the apartment has been slightly broken by the faint bluish illumination that emerges from behind the bedside tables, which are suspended in the air, and is softly projected over the floor in a manner reminiscent of the maritime atmospheres that characterize this project. On the right, a mirror makes the space appear appreciably larger.

The use of metal in the shower, and its overall design, reflect a boat, the original inspiration of the project.

The glass door between the living room and the terrace is barely noticeable and allows the view of the sea to be enjoyed. A balustrade on the terrace gives the sensation of being on the deck of a boat.

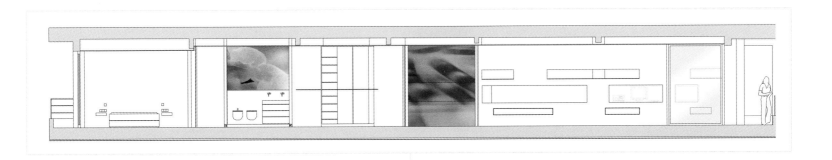

The studio has been designed as a multifunctional space that can be converted into a guest room. In the bathroom, a screen decorated with jellyfish illuminates and decorates the space and gives the room a futurist air.

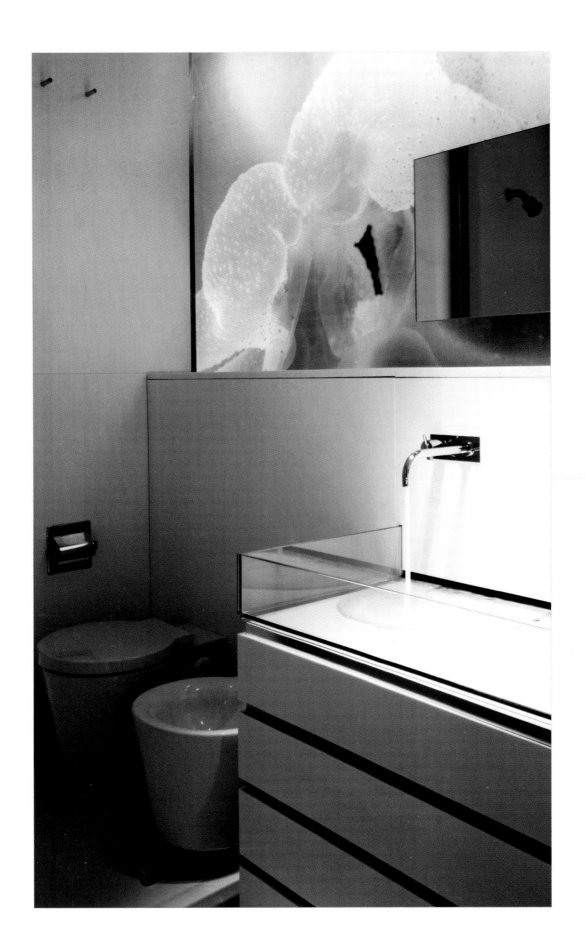

A House on a Slope

Two critical factors influenced this project: its location and the clients' requirements. The house is situated on a slope with views of the Lake of Zurich in Switzerland.

The residence is oriented in such a way that the front enjoys the best views while the back enjoys more sunlight. However, the floor plan has been designed in such a way that allows light to penetrate into the northern part of the house and also so that the landscape can be contemplated from the far side of the residence.

As a result of eliminating some walls, greater communication flows between the public and private spaces inside the house and between the building and its surroundings. Large windows integrate the outside with the inside to such an extent that one seems to imitate the other. The walls covered with different materials and the diversity of floorings distinguish each area within the large open space.

The different zones are arranged according to function have been kept together on one floor. Some of the furnishings have been integrated into the architectural structure of the building and fulfill the dual purpose of dividers and storage elements ■

Right, a detail of one of the separating elements, which has been made in a translucent material to allow the light through and which also connects the living area with the kitchen.

Above, the original design of this space and its illumination create an atmosphere that is both avant-garde and luminous.

Some built-in shelves also fulfill the function of separating zones.

The staircase that bridges the two levels stands out due to its steel handrail.

A house in the Netherlands

This house forms part of a residential development in Borneo Sporenburg, east of Amsterdam. The studio West 8 Landscape Architects have designed the urban development of this area. The way in which the plots have been divided into elongated parcels, and in which the buildings have been arranged in rows, could not be more typical of this particular area.

Each sixteen-and-a-half-foot-wide piece of land contains a house made up of an elongated band to which, on different floors, one or two spaces have been annexed. One of these is dedicated to a guest room with bathroom. The other accommodates two studios, one on the first level and the other on the second. The remaining areas of the residence can be distributed in various ways.

The most elongated part of the building is formed by a glazed structure from which two volumes hang at different heights. A small alley for private use has been created below the volumes. In addition to the two volumes, a third element has been incorporated. A box installed below the height of the street and over which a cover has been inclined fulfills the function of an entrance ramp for the parking facilities. The design of the construction allows light in through the large windows that form the roof ■

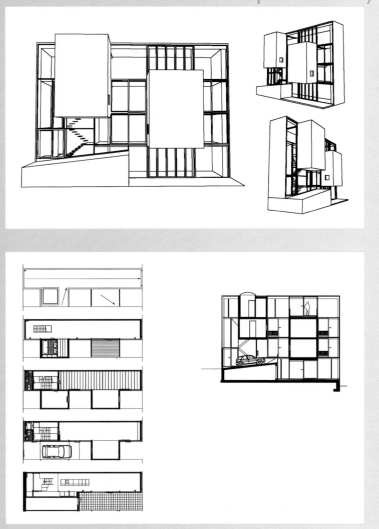

Above, various sections of the floor plan, in which we can see how the closed volumes are combined with the glazed areas. The interior spaces are easily viewed from the outside.

The rustic wooden flooring creates a relaxing atmosphere. The use of traditional elements in the interior contrasts with the innovative design of the exterior of the house.

Open Spaces and Intimacy

This family residence in New York is the result of combining two apartments. The architects were commissioned to open up the space as much as possible and to adapt it to the family's needs without losing the privacy of each of the zones.

The space is organized around three different areas. The formal area is comprised of the living room, the dining room, an open-plan kitchen, the reception area, and a guest room. The private areas are comprised of the office and bedrooms and bathroom. The master suite is formed by a bedroom, bathroom, and a balcony. The team of Cho Slade achieved a perfect relationship between the domestic and private areas.

The furniture in the three zones is made of sycamore wood, which confers unity on the whole. Only in some carefully selected elements have new materials, such as leather, stone, or glass, been introduced. The windows were also remodeled to make the most of natural light and to enable the magnificent views of the city to be enjoyed ■

The kitchen is situated in the formal area and is open to the dining room, living room, guest room, and reception area. The space has been organized around the furniture and glass panels to preserve the autonomy of each area.

Classic materials, such as marble in different cream tones, are combined with dark-colored metals to enrich the whole with different textures and contrasts.

Synthesis with Tradition

The location of this residence on the outskirts of Galway, a rural area, allowed the team of professionals from Mark Guard Architects to deepen their investigations into the traditional Irish house in non-urban areas. The result is a synthesis between traditional and modern elements according to the needs of the family that inhabits the house.

Simplicity is the most important aspect of the project, but not at a loss to the application of interesting new ideas, whether formal or related to the organization of the space. A good example of this is the distribution of the different zones of the house, which is far from what could be considered conventional.

The children's rooms are situated on the ground floor to give them direct access to the garden. The living room, however, is found upstairs so as to make the most of the natural light available, the height of the ceilings, and the views.

The organization of the interior space stands out for its great versatility. Sliding panels allow the areas to be enlarged or subdivided as necessary. Some of the house's original fittings have been preserved, which creates a welcoming and elegant atmosphere ■

minimalist airs

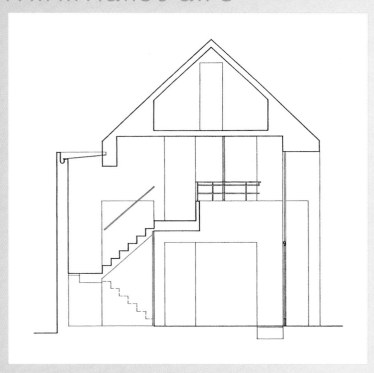

The whites, the light-colored wooden flooring, and the absence of superfluous elements create an austere atmosphere.

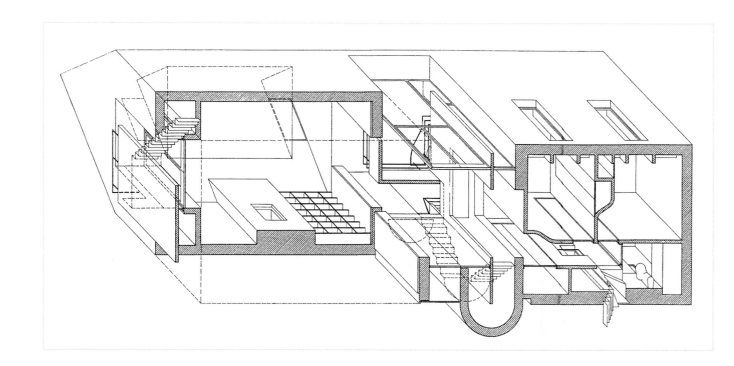

A House in Notting Hill

In this undertaking by Seth Stein Architects, great importance has been given to the relationship between the space and the materials used. These elements have been enriched by other aspects, such as the lighting. Formal design and innovative spaces typify the work of this team of architects. In this case, on the upper floor, a skylight has been included to improve the natural illumination and, so as not to lose any usable space, access has been created between the rooms situated below the skylight, with both the balustrade and the floor constructed of glass so that a maximum amount of sunlight can flow in.

The architecture of this residence, constructed in Notting Hill, London, is anything but usual in this neighborhood. The white walls and curved roof contrast with the brick buildings that are more typical of the area. The lie of the land and the patio, which was constructed later, determined the design of the construction, which includes a small office as requested by the clients. An L-shaped floor plan has been organized around an open-air space. In the longest wing a special spatial sequence has been generated from where the views can be enjoyed. The large glazed surfaces that enclose the areas oriented toward the patio open them up to this space ■

In the plans for the house, we can see the L-shaped floor plan that is organized around an interior patio. The regulations for urban development in this area permit constructions of two levels along with an additional level modeled within the profile of the roof.

On the right, the bathroom stands out for its simplicity and for the absence of accessories. The colors are of similar tones, unifying the elements and creating an appearance of a unique space.

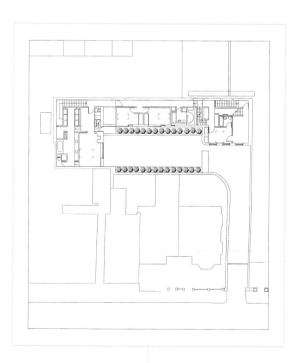